Feasts of Devotion

Feasts of Devotion

Snowdon Barnett

Rivelin Grapheme Press

First published in 2010 by Rivelin Grapheme Press, The Pavilion, 10 Inkpen Road, Kintbury (Near Newbury), Berkshire, RG17 9TU, England

10 9 8 7 6 5 4 3 2 1

© Snowdon Barnett 2010 whose right to be identified as the author of this work has been asserted in accordance with Sections 88 and 78 of the Copyright Designs and Patents Act 1988.

Snowdon's work can be obtained from Rivelin Grapheme Press at jsb@snowdonbarnett.com

All rights reserved. No part of this publication may be reproduced, stored in a retrieval system or transmitted in any form or by any means, electronic, mechanical, photocopying, recording, digital or otherwise, without the prior written permission of the author.

A CIP catalogue record for this book is available from the British Library.

ISBN 978-0-947612-41-2

Printed and bound in England by The Lavenham Press.

Contents

Preface   vii

Part One   1

bring back to the way   3
*Nineteen Poems
of fusion to benediction*

Part Two   47

five small loaves   49

Seven Sonnets of Use & Abuse   53
Praises   63
Ruth   73
Canticles   83
Revelation   93

Part Three   103

19 recent *Nineteen Liners*   105

Part Four   129

Coda : *Appearances*   131

Poetry published by Snowdon Barnett

Lines on the Colour Turquoise (*an autobiographical lyric*)	Oriel Press (Routledge Kegan Paul) London	1979
Last Entry (*a Romance of Antarctica and Captain R F Scott*)	Oriel Press (as above)	1982
Lapis Lazuli (*vexato quaestio*)	Grapheme Publications London	1983
Dossiers Secrets (*a Gnostic tract in verse*) with *The Argument*, published simultaneously	Rivelin Grapheme Press London	1986
Hiroshima Hypostasis (*a poem for the Millenium*)	Mellen Poetry Press New York, Ontario & London	1997
Poetry Chapbook (*a choice from forty years of writing Verse*)	Hilton House Norwich, England	2000
Once in a Blue Moon (*my BiMillennium Poem*)	Mellen Poetry Press (as above)	2003
Now is as it pitches (*reflective lyric*)	Mellen Poetry Press (as above)	2004
Nocturne (*devotional and prayer-poems*)	Rivelin Grapheme Press (as above)	2006

Preface

> *Feasts of Devotion are certain festivals, the observance of which is not obligatory, but is "left to the devotion of the faithful." The observance of such feasts is therefore supposed to be specially meritorious* [1]

In this Preface I set out how this Collection came into being, make a mention of the illustrations and conclude with some general comments.

Although my Devotional Work has its origins in parts of *Hiroshima Hypostasis* which was composed during 1996, the first relevant collection is *Once in a Blue Moon* which germinated in Old Goa over Easter 1999 and became my millennium-reflective.

My mother died after a dis-spiriting illness and in her death there was much sadness as she revealed to me her own lifetime's crucial mistakes and how in her innocence and loyalty (which were two of her attractive features) she had been let down by some of those she had held close. In short she had made *wrong choices* and I was drawn into a consideration of my own.

Accordingly, after her funeral on *All Halloes Eve* 2003 up to Boxing Day 2004 I wrote that which became *bring back to the way* (a quotation from Gerard Manley Hopkins), in which I explore how and why I chose to move closer from the Gnosticism of my 1986 *Dossiers Secrets* into that mysticism which pervades my poems of 2006 in *Nocturne*. In this, now Part One, I tread a path to where poems may come from and in accompanying prose notes written contemporaneously with the verse which sits opposite, I trace some of my steps.

My Father died on 12th April 2006 and in his memory I put together 5 complimentary pieces, being reflections on parts of the *Holy Bible* which I call *five small loaves* being (as Part Two): *Seven Sonnets of Use & Abuse*
Praises
Ruth
Canticles
Revelation
which were all in some form of existence at that time.

Following upon *Nocturne*, I continued to write my *Nineteen Liners* and it is another 19 of those which comprises Part Three.

As I was approaching closure of this Collection I decided to add a *Coda* being my sixty six line poem *Appearances*. It is not without interest that *Appearances* has evolved into *An Easter Trilogy*, being three verse plays as first, a description of their special home in *Bethany*, secondly the *Trial of Jesus* and third his *Appearances* into *Parousia:* but that is for another time. In summary, Parts One and Three are myself looking inwards, while reaching outwards is the theme of those other two.

These are devotional pieces which are not intended to be devoured at one sitting. This is a table spread for your refreshment to visit as you wish. It is a board constantly replenished and, if promised, proffers sustenance which will be made available as I illustrate here by *bring back to the way*, which was anticipated in the *Preface* to *Nocturne*, being now presented. As I have recorded elsewhere, my work is some continuum. Maybe I have been too apologetic in the past as to its purport.

In the arrangement of these poems I have not been concerned with dates of composition. Rather, I have commenced with explanation, moved to examination, paused as at an exhibition in order to end with exhilaration. And, so, I have planted my garden but there is no prohibition as to which fruit you may pick first.

As to the illustrations, I explain on page 44 why there are capitals to the prose notes in Part One and I thank my brother, Winston, not only for the illuminations, but also for selecting the type face which is used throughout, *Book Antiqua* in Point 11. Those Capitals appear to *float* which I think is some counterpoint to *walking on water*.

For the illustrations in Part Two I have chosen photographs of the six churches which are within my local Benefice :
Page 52   St Michael and All Angels at Enborne
Page 62   St Mary's at Hampstead Marshall
Page 72   St Lawrence's at West Woodhay
Page 82   St Swithun's at Coombe
Page 92   St Michael's at Inkpen
Page 102   St Mary the Virgin at Kintbury with Avington

I employ those because they illustrate to me *a spirit of place*. I am not a communicant of the Church of England, only a disciple who continues to disappoint my Lord. I thank Derek Clements for establishing the copyright ownership in these illustrations and through him Philip Wilson for that on Page 102 and Sarah Luton for the other five.
For the concept of the layout of the notes which preface each of the five sections in Part Two, I acknowledge *The London Cruciform Lectionary*[2].

I place throughout six coloured photographs of my brother's recent sculptures which he makes by hand. That on page 128 of *David & Jonathan* is in situ in my garden in Kintbury, *God is Great* at page 130 was built in collaboration with Roger Stonehouse in his garden in Togston and *Adam & Eve* at page 106 stands in my brother's garden in Charlton, also in Northumberland where the other three, which are free standing can be viewed namely page 2 *Gerard Manley Hopkins*, page 48 the *Lord Jesus Christ* and page 104 *Paul & Apollos*.

I end this Collection at Part Four with a line drawing on page 141 which is similar to those which he provided for my first book *Lines on the Colour Turquoise* and which provides a closing connection.

If, in the run of text, I mention names but do not add specific references, it is because I assume familiarity : if that offends, then I apologise. Also, at this point, I wish to thank Nina Clark for her patience in typing out my manuscript and MC Patel for his support throughout.

I have been asked why I published *Nocturne* through my own Press. I did so because I believed it worth publishing and apart from one dissenting voice it has been well received. Rivelin Grapheme Press has published 75 volumes of verse and some 139 poets of whom I am only one. It seems to me that with texting and twittering the whole conception of *publication* has changed forever into something Gutenberg would never have envisaged. This volume may now represent a state of being "in line" before going "on line".

I prepare this *Preface* with this Collection complete. I am conscious of its diversity and that appreciation may be problematic for a reader navigating the whole in one sailing as these poems are from various ports of call. They are, as another said of his first collection :
> "poems so materially different from those upon which general approbation is at present bestowed"[3]

that I consider it appropriate to add these comments. I accept that these four sections are different but this is a *Feast* and it is proper that each course provides multiple flavours to satiate different palates.

I go further and accept that my several collections contrast from each other not just in form and structure but in content and meaning. This is not an ageing process: it concerns different times of day and, consequently, something of some night.

There is displayed here a fusion of thought through prayer. Each breath as a feast of fellowship. There is hope presented in these poems so that that which is temporarily occluded may become revealed.

> *I have heard in that fierce embrace, even*
> *the gods speak of God*[4]

and so abandon any concept of *God* being some external : this is internal. Do not explore outside; investigate within. Place the whole of your experience around these poems and permit spirits to move together into their wholeness of understanding.

I've avoided throughout my writing criticising the work of any other poet or even commenting upon their work because a poem exists in its own shape and form: it occupies its own existence quite separate from any poet. How do critics who are not poets deign to judge a poem's length and breadth, its weight or value: *never mind the quality feel the width,* as someone repeated.

I add something about verse generally before it may all just e-mail itself away on faceless texts. Has anyone considered Lord Byron, suffused, in his cups, not enabled to put pen to paper but feeling free to finger-surf the web: how prolix *Childe Harold* then? Moving on to Lowell's *Notebooks* which are now obviously much too short, lacking a daily diarrhoea of twittering.

So, rather than criticising, I prefer to state where I stand as one grain in this sand-storm of verse because I feel there is poetry in everyday, through everything, and, more, in everyone. There is a need for Poetry as there is a desire for Belief and, beyond that, a certainty in Faith.

There is a time for composition and another for appreciation; going onwards in to that holy time for reading with comprehension, to memorizing for reciting, even, perhaps, advancing into listening.

There may be another time, precisely an attempt to formulate, to analyse. An immediate problem with this stage is that there is no template for that exercise. Verse exists: I say, let it be. Critics emerge: I add, let them be gone.

Poetry must first of all engage, next it should explicate, finally it needs to entertain : unbind our tied-up bodies, release our souls, free our spirits into realms of verse; refresh faces with dews of morning – a new day – a verse day – a birthday.

Poems open doors into a reality of being, escaping unreality which is the dross of daily-ness. When I open my eyes to a morning's brightness, I begin again, once more afresh, forgiving of a night-times fleshfulness. To be pure : to consider my world as something in need of saving (perhaps redeeming) and to appreciate that none of that is capable of fulfilment if I have not myself entered into some state of grace, holiness, contentment.

One of the advantages of activating this medium of verse is that there is no impediment to presenting in one poem an idea or theory or concept which may appear to be quite incompatible with that which may have been displayed in another poem, without suffering any pang of conscience or feeling any sense of contrition or remorse.

Another purpose of writings such as these must be to assist others in their journey on their own way. In a wayside Inn, evening, resting by a bar, *Traveller* turning his back from the door, not ajar, seeks solace. That *solace* is a prime purpose of these poems. It seeks to illustrate a path through and out of any wood of doubt.

My work is to place on a page shadows passing. Poetry is a source of light inside myself which may enable me to illuminate some other life.

I do not feel I can have a move apposite closure to this *Preface* than to quote *The Opening*.[5]

In the name of God,
Merciful to all,
Compassionate to each!

Praise be to God, Lord of the Worlds:
Merciful to all,
Compassionate to each!
Lord of the Day of Judgement.
It is You we worship, and upon You we call for help.
Guide us to the straight path,
The path of those upon whom Your grace abounds,
Not those upon whom anger falls,
Nor those who are lost.

Snowdon Barnett, Kintbury, 7th March 2010

---

[1] *The Protestant Dictionary*, New and Revised Edition, C. Sydney Carter and G.E. Alison Weeks, The Harrison Trust, London 1933.
[2] From *Sacred* edited by John Reeves, British Library 2007.
[3] The Preface to *Lyrical Ballads*, William Wordsworth, Second Edition January 1801 (in two volumes containing the Preface).
[4] *Self-Portrait* from *River Flow,* David Whyte, Many Rivers Press, Washington 2007.
[5] *The Qur'an* a new translation by Tarif Khalidi, Penguin Classics London 2008.
[6] Winston Barnett's work is accessible at www.winstonbarnettart.com
His painting of the Castle on the *Holy Island* of Lindisfarne is reproduced on the cover.

Part One

Gerard Manley Hopkins

bring back to the way

*Nineteen Poems
of fusion to benediction*

In this collection of nineteen poems, of nineteen lines each, I am attempting to restrict (if not remove altogether) the use of the definite and indefinite article. To do so, I maintain, adds focus: removes the *umms* and *ahhs* besetting talk. It also introduces another opportunity for *studied deviation* except, that is, where the definite helps the general rhythm with an internal rhyme. Also, there is no punctuation, only breathing.

And another thing, my father, whom God preserve, suggested (and, I believe, quite sensibly) that I should notate each poem because it is easier to perceive landscape after mists of doubt dispel: another chain line on laid paper. These prose additions form three paragraphs each and therefore are their own prose poem

I have centred each poem on the right hand page but blocked the prose notes to the left: the balance is the 10th line of the poem which sits opposite a capital; therefore they should be read as counterpoint, not dissimilar to my setting of *Lapis Lazuli*. The central phrase is from Bernard Levin resuming his column after *The Times'* problems as these poems reflect stopping and re-starting. The working title of this collection was *Nineteen* but I have taken the present from *Notes on Suarez, De Mysteriis Vitae Christi* by Gerard Manley Hopkins

Contents

A	introductory	4
B	farewell	7
C	Lord's Prayer	9
D	Demiurge	11
E	unless the meaning of sheep unfolds	13
F	by blakelaw farm	15
G	VERTICALITY	17
H	snownessly	19
I	from their North	21
K	for those Jews	23
L	some Tenth	25
M	9/11	27
N	beyond a labyrinth	29
O	third eye of knowing	31
P	soul journey	33
Q	looking through lawns	35
R	doorway	37
S	bewilderment	39
T	caudal clause	41
V	Nineteen	43
Y	end-piece	44
	Dedication	46

Running from but contained within is a fusion of the work of GMH and Dylan Marlais Thomas, poets interested in poems, not poetry. I add no more: I leave that concept to develop, to expand as other pieces fall in place, into my lap, waiting as I am under this greenwood tree. One thing I will state in relation to these poems is that in respect of GMH I will eschew the use of his favoured word *things*.

By chance this has become the first of a sequence of, I think at the present, 19 poems of 19 lines in which each poem will spin on the pin of the central and tenth line. It was written on Boxing Day 2003, the year closing my mother's death, the day after her anticipated 89th birthday.

I use *fouetté* which is a ballet-step in which a foot makes a whip-like motion, for me, the kick of death or, as with the last word, Mum's favourite, candy, just melting away. The whole carries an autumnal aura but it is only sorrowful not sad: that time for pressing fruits to flavour which I have done through many seasons. A ritual that refreshes throughout long winters.

farewell
(a poem of passing)

fascinate firm greenwood trees
full foison formed of crops from seed
soft winds which peace of spring may fruit
her slowly saraband surprise safe shrubbery
astonishing as leaves abate

three tasty mushrooms by high faery moss
queasy from quaffing cydre
over-grieving rent pavilions of hearts
smashed on corms of oddities
farewell fouetté
autumn's yellowing sallows
weather whispering wintery from west
wanword onto her secret copse

refocilate by slow trickling stream
salves and treacles either pills or potions
arms akimbo in her picnic fest
summer pudding of a dress
rubescent firelight evanesce
such energy with everything discandy

As well as the three references in Mathew, Mark and Luke to the prayer on the Mount of Olives, I have conjoined the *Prayer of Jesus* in John 17 with the lyrical *Song of Moses* in Deuteronomy 32, which it supersedes. This is to be contrasted with the familiarity of the Disciples' prayer which has become more of a mantra and has moved far from a Rabbi's reminder of the three keystones as in John 6 v 9-13.

hoosing this Hopkins/Thomas fusion, I've deliberately abandoned the convention of capitals for the trinity, save for the intercessor, the *Holy Spirit*. Writing in the shadow of the poetry of the Geneva Bible (which Shakespeare used) may be daunting but holds its own rewards.

All the line ends rhyme somewhere with another, although some do so but softly except the aforementioned advocate (as the law would have it). That provides the fulcrum of the central line and so has no position to cover, to move into the parlance of the beautiful game. I've opened up the poem from garden down to seashore, ie the place to leave, with the reference to Matthew Arnold's *Dover Beach*, ignoring Anthony Hecht's *Dover Bitch*.

Lord's Prayer
(an invocation)

Father
this cup refuse
your will dispose

through agonies of earnestness
angel's buttress
sweating great clots of gore
fulfil with grieving sorrow Arnold's emptied shore

finishing this work you charged me
your word through truth to sanctify
placing with my disciples your Paraclete
attuning *Song of Moses* this new plea
by your peace resuming my place eternity

revealing your name
through those who choose to stay
who watch to pray
for those who yearn to love and so remain

Father
your hour has come
to glorify your son

That search for some *eternal something*, that ideal excellence striving within each one, must be continued: I show it by reference to the supernatural. In an appreciation of those, that higher nature will be made manifest. It may appear that references to GMH overmount DMT; that is not so; Dylan's mostly words are here, scattered as seeds, *bones*, *green*, *marrow* and *thighs*.

emiurge contemplates that mass of creation which is too great for my human soul to comprehend, especially as some small particle of the *Infinite Soul* is lodged in each of us, call it *divine spark, spiritual ego*, whatever.

In this central line I try to confront myself. With that in mind, consider the scythe which I combine into the cylindrical of *trephine*. It is this which strives us onwards to do our best, *Ishwara* being a symbol of *logos* that *Higher Self* to which all must aspire. It is the sun in his sky at noonday's brilliance. In this fusion it should be remembered that GMH considered himself half-Welsh. *instress* is one of his special words: the stress within, that which unifies thoughts into meaningness.

Demiurge
(for Ishwara)

knuckle beneath deep purple skies as sprinkling rains kiss
cool winds chill moon's sharp shaft
as stern gods hole heaven's one clear spot
suddenly revealing Cyclopes' power of pure command
thunder lightning thunderbolt

wave date-palm leaves by tamarisk tree
fountains of truth designing to deluge
husbandmen harvesting fruits for spirits free-wheeling
bees celestial food suffused with truth

instressing indwelling self

friends dancing nymphs fly heavenly fiends
sacred white elephant
steers buccaneers into pools of peace
right hand to rudder turns Isis' papyrus boat
hitching rigging laddering evil
breakers of night seas reflecting spin stars

through vapour smoke trephine through thorn or thistle
in thirsty worlds scour vineyards first

cockerels crowing full moonshine all night long

This is a poem on the passing of school-friend Barbara (toots) Elliot in New York on 14 November 2003 which I wrote when another friend, John Dunn, heard and told me in late January 2004. It is deliberately focused on myself which, I hope, might help others if they mirror themselves in a not dissimilar situation: hoping to but not meeting.

veryone is important but some become more so than others. The message of the poem contained in the central trio is that once the hand at the wheel stops spinning there may be no more. Address the weaver before it's too late, especially when their given years are less than yours.

The *jar* refers to the poem in 1 Kings 17 v 14 concerning Elijah and the widow at Zarephath (the continuance of meeting):
> *jar of meal shall not be spent*
> *jug of oil shall not be emptied*

The *Golden Spinning Wheel* is one of Dvorak's symphonic poems, filled with lightness and grace.

unless the meaning of sheep unfolds
(a poem of loss)

too muchly this embroidery
for living through experienced forgetfulness
assuming at homecoming Sidon's jar fulfilled

into an alabaster box I hoard my heart's cord
interlace her *Golden Spinning Wheel* as I ease her latch
memories as sepia folded on worn chests
photographs fade from whittling frames
dust settling silvery grate

span scarcely stretch
spinning as idling lilies leave
knowing nor cleft nor weave

voices at 'phones echo unanswered quiescence
where ear prints uniqueness archaize
her *Lost Chord* forever

only shadows of clouds sweeping hay fields
all sense burnt off
with hopes of harvest withering
touching shrouds to personal mortalities
snorting at snowflakes too early for firedrakes

In this poem I describe the *situs* but look through it to the transience of human change as re-arrangement of standing stones. I've repeated the end*ing* to piece the poem together; although it has not the sufficiency of *fusion* which I seek, I leave it alone as that stepping stone across water. It's meant to be a poem spoken while walking uphill: - a series of short breaths. And what happens on home-coming? We sup with family and friends – this is for my brother, Winston, homing from the Antipodes.

riendship is simplistic: a still, single, small window giving a changing view outside to landscape, sheep and clouds drifting by: weary age watching a shepherd lad at work. Here (and elsewhere) I try to follow Dylan using epithets to surprise.

As I consider my life in cycles of 19, ignoring my first 7 years to December 1949, gives me a 1st cycle to 1968 when I was 26, a 2nd to 1987 at age 45 and this 3rd (which still runs) up to 2006 *When I'm 64.* I cannot envisage a 4th to 2025 and being 83 years of old! Although, as I write, my father enjoys his 91st year of grace. It poses the question of mobility: will I still be travelling in the body then or only by the spirit of my mind, desk-bound and library encased.

by blakelaw farm
(a poem for homecoming)

my travelling clothes limp-lining by latch-key
dry-stone walling wandering horizon
distance is a quarry of bracked bones

place-name for blackening out-cropped coal
or simpler night-shadings of heather

staring southerly wind-worsening westerly
clouds covering blinds drawing windows
shuttering Cheviot's ice-slicing
cries chase of slender shapes off skittish hills
stains rough River Rede red peat
fat pheasants' reluctance for feast
wandering downstream with black-faced sheep

robbing landscapes resting to rural
by those leisure led whilst observant beasts
rut through familiarities
croppings of carrot not nipped by rabbit
mulches to soup with trout not mink-nicked

settling a griddle for dropped scones
breaking bread for blessings for brotherhood

Now I am concerned with that point in each life when struck down, laid low, *Verticality* becomes a state past far horizons: that epiphanic moment. It began simply as the she-moon and he-sun but lines too closely bound together swiftly lose meaning. When the moon is overhead it is much more manageable than as white disc rising an horizon. Problems at first sight materialize as enormous shape: settling beneath them, they wane.

ermination has its own slow process. In the high summer of 2003, long before this sequence, my brother planted this concept but it did not energize until 25 January 2004 when I sojourned with him. This poem encourages looking above, upwards, outwards, forwards: indeed, in any direction except to that infernal, an internal.

Posing a series of questions, tempting a reader's response, it became much too serious and now contrasts the very upright GMH with a more laid-back (no pun intended) DMT: vertical to horizontal. Perhaps they are not too far distant: is *Spelt from Sibyl's Leaves* so much away from those studied deviations of Thomas such as the phrase *All the sun long* in *Fern Hill*. This is for Patricia, who understandeth.

VERTICALITY
(a poem approaching clarity)

concerning Saint Paul's conversion
some street subbed straight draws blinds but lightly
overhead moon's reducing sphere faces full facing edge
emasculating make-up to night musk

as to this Perpendicular
marrowing low-life to high-life through no-life
condensation peels bills from perforations
architects as artichokes are resting arthrospore

printers struggling to predicate *p's* and *q's*
amending orthographie
attesting witnesses focus font's lacunae

all ago through grieves of studious deviation
high style oscillates originality
rustic quoins traduce Sam Plimsoll's line

soaring zenethian mackerel sky
past eagle's weak-livering Promethean shaft
locate light refract incandescence
as sunsets spread horizons butterfly
vault unswerving verticality

A snow-bound night in West Woodburn, Northumberland where I could not return to the Inn for my belongings but in the morning was driven along a disused railway track to Woolsington Airfield so I could turn South. An old friend, the present land worker and owner, drove me and my daughter Daisy out in his four-wheeler: so this is for Terence, his home poem.

ere is a made-up word: if I can't find one then I make one up because words must start sometime, someplace, somehow. The structure is:
picture/reflection
pause
picture/ refraction.

As this poem reflects a particular incident I've tried to make it ever-present by using once again the repetition of *ing*. The 11th Commandment is given by Jesus at John 8 v 34/35 in the *Farewell Discourses*. In rescue remedy there is a reference to a combination of five Bach *Remedies*, recommended for effecting calm. Things are rarely as they seem: it is pointless to resist change.

snownessly
(a poem of promise of rescue)

elements contrive to fold me to this snow place
as sheep nestle windfall off wind falling flakes
choosing snowed in from snowed out
worrying for animals feeding no watering

my concern's for souls distilled not fulfilled
commandment eleven *love one another* embracing
all others and comers through marquetry
whole carpentry refixing lives' broken artefact

away is some heart place distant many suns
attending for listening rescue remedy
retrocede and children of delight revanche

wood burning slow grate unlocking gold key
cabinets of secrets night flickering guests
Bay Horse noisiest on attendance in trough
longering valleys foot-spread years lengthening

traducing this chalice for those ornithoid awaiting
snowdrops to daffies with crocus first springers'
chorus so far removed as rambutan
snow-blinking ascending saints blocking off narrowings

Today, Mothering Sunday, and my first without my mother, I am reminded of Elaine who lost hers joylessly last year and who gave me a selection of Kathleen Ferrier, my mum's favourite, which has been both comfort and solace as I prepare lunch for Daisy's mum, Elizabeth Ann. It is also the first day of Spring and therefore all in all this is most pointedly for *Klever Kaff* whom I never met but meet each time she sings because her song is for each one of us in our separate aloneness.

I am in this odd day, cool but bright with blossom touching shrubs and smaller trees. 33 years ago today, also a Sunday, I collapsed at about four in the afternoon, later, quite much later, to be diagnosed with the young man's disease, Crohn's and face several ops of an unpleasantness not notated in the annals of the Bellona Club.

On reflection, those echoes of *Blow the Wind Southerly* and *What is Life* became my first musical influence. I was ten when she died in 1953 but it was not until 1957 that I arrived at Charlie Gracie's *It's Fu Fu Fabulous* which turned me through other discords. *harrowing* (*of hell*) is Christ's deliverance of the souls of those faithful patriarchs and prophets as described in the *Descencus ad Inferos*. Life is our gift, its continuance my bonus. I have employed it not uncannily.

from their North
(a poem dissembling)

there stills as slight as fluff amongst flax clouds
rising full ring to spread through globes as gossamer
shivers of promises falling off her frame
fumbling art's state from grace
arms and their armours all abased
through strength of song liberalizing full loving lives

as suddenly comes face to window beckoning back door alas
fireside emptied with blackened grate to coldness
no longer sing they together never evermore

philosophy thighs untying of knots from notes

no more tallies for this journeyman northwards
scenting of heathers aphelion zaffre fainting bluishness
no more for *Keel Row* than blanchey son a-shine
Come you not from Newcastle? whence canny magpies migrate
failing to tidy detritus from youth's wastage

listening hard for masterly blowing of train's whistle
leaving my station where stand homesteads
sea-breakers promising salt-spray off tears
what of harrowing whilst song decomposes heartlands

This poem has become a reflection on the position of Jews in history, now possibly becoming more relevant in the context of Mel Gibson's controversial film *The Passion of Christ* if there is to be some anti-semitic reaction to it. I began this during Jewish Book Week 2004, but it has turned into a diffident poem – as if I were leading a goat into some wilderness, disputing the need for nationality: why should homeland affect who I am or what I do?

Knowing friends who tread the maternal Jewish pathway has been one of the fruits of my life especially as I emerged from a patricianhood of Plymouth Brethren. Thus, I would have preferred this to be in the dyadic line, the one from Hebrew which contains two parallels but I've failed.

This mixture germinates from a review in the TLS of Charles Murray's book *Human Accomplishment* which was followed by reading A C Grayling's essay *Anti-Semitism and The Holocaust* from his *The Mystery of Things*. Are not all notions a broth? Finally *anguis fragilis* is the much misunderstood earthworm, a species of lizard and *diaspora* as used here is in that generality of dispersion whether of people, language or cultures. Much discourse ensued from GMH expounding *sweetheart* in a sermon.

for those Jews
(a diaspora)

upon this rock set foot from softly sandy seas
tempt sorely shell-shore wanderings
Ebionite settling Davidic dance
Jesu sage tempt magician's magic sane
unity of spirit prescribing bounds of peace

at afternoon prayers bending doubling glimpse
tsitsit's spiritual silkiness concealing woollen working togs
mezuza declares belief
bloodied door posts bestride grateful hearth warmth

robes of glory

unresting dove-tailed tongued and grooved
counterpoint to discourse reasoning kindness
crassly uncertain citing Halacha
no need of homestead for a world at home

if only skins were shed as easy *anguis fragilis*
being neither blind nor slow but worming upwards grace
in dew-soaked herbiage sound sense is all defence

from a majority of persecution soften minorities to sweethearts
wanderers beyond frontiers captives to wonderment

These prose pages are falling into their own form being a general opening or linking comment, the centre focusing on the poem itself around the Capital and the third closing with specific words or phrases used. I have sought towards a completeness, regarding this collection as some wholeness. It is, after all, in memory of a life and as such individual parts may easily be misconstrued.

Letters are no more important than numbers and this poem is concerned with a lettering of the number *ten*. Although written 7th in order of composition it is the central 10th. Therefore the key to the whole sequence is the 10th line: *through gardens of reeds* being line 182 out of the total (ignoring the titles) of 363 lines of verse.

gardens of reeds is a symbol of the astral plane containing *Summerland*, where from its papyrus swamps the *Self* emerges to display its own *Individuality* in order to achieve union between those higher and lower levels: this is the central point of existence. There are shadows painted in these poems of ironies which lie outside the frame, perhaps the ghost of the poet, the plight of William Nicholson.

some Tenth
(non-digital numerology)

drifting onto dry land stampeding tundra
elephantine monsters slaying from slush seas
clothed with cosmic carapace
balancing incense in wonder
light brightest shimmering transient cascades

from rain forests timbering top-tables
by tip-time pure maths not readily applied
numbering amazement in arms-giving
tapping barometers at fashion's daily drop-out

through *gardens of reeds* through

sacred number of natural perfection
shining between candlesticks calibrating stars
ten lepers washing outside their tenth month
embalming ethers of perception on their pause

olive groves' soma tree of lives
he-goat she-mounting ego's inspiration
tortoise shedding shell's reality
amulets crafted by blesséd holy hands
leviathan stand by

I use this poem as a springboard to hope, future, all of the beautiful. The opposite of this quote:
> *you (that's me) love life*
> *we (that's some sad soul) love death.*

Well! I'm for living and if *Terror* ends mine, I'll die living not living to die. Panic is an open door to oppression, an excuse for suppressing free speech. It is another manifestation of terrorism.

adrid 3/11 compelled me to revisit the Twin Towers: an image depicting that demon lurking throughout *Twin Peaks*. To begin with the making of some sense I reduce these to their basic number 2: symbolizing the duality of manifestation; one becomes two, spirit and matter, good or evil.

I resist writing gore on gore. I was unable to respond to New York 9/11 because of its sudden ferocity. The accumulation of violence since has, peculiarly, enabled me to regard those horrors face-on. The central word *gardyloo* is that cry in Edinburgh for those passing below to avoid the contents of the piss-pot: anarchists above, workers below, case rests.

The quotation is attributed to Abu Dujan al-Afghani, a spokesman for al-Quaeda after Madrid, Times, 20 March 2004 (I have added the words in brackets).

9/11
(fury against formlessness)

peacefully gardens flowering
threatening terror from error
strangling life from all merrie humours
immersing earth's natural blue skies
spiriting truth from falsehood's sprite

none other than blindworms' rank damp ditch
on a sultry day one spray from cloudlessness
shovelling molehill disturbing buzzards
armies of worms garlicky vegetarians beware

gardyloo

entrancing xian from warehouses thrust thus far west
from Yemen's illicit enchantments
such many no longer by harbourside distancing touch
pieces of peace falling piecemeal fail entirely

way for life or wage of death
fresh bloodied fauna & flora dripping wildnesses
eviscerate with fire drawn scimitar
deracinate each tree for every hope for growth despoil
law may only be fulfilled through love

Consider this journey as climbing a mountain: to report success it is essential to negotiate a successfully pre-planned descent. In maturer years it is that descent which rounds off the journey: something for others not to emulate (for each must make their own) but to consider. In this journey bide not only overnight but have a rest-day, enjoy comfort stops (and more) during each day. Employ as many holy-days as you may.

othing betters C L R James' *Beyond a Boundary*. There is no jump from prose to poetry, but, alas, there is backsliding the other way. These two are mighty dragons which must never fight. Slaying each other from afar, each retreats through her own valley, into her cave of choice.

If I use *His* then I fall into a sexist trap. When I use *God*, I espouse monotheism. Therefore, I need to focus upon a neutral word for this concept: I've invented *goodsenseness*. This poem is for my oldest surviving London friend from the Sixties, Michael Hagi Soteri, a believer. I wrote it after he explained to me the specialness of one of his many visits to Mount Athos and the monastic republic there which may embrace a pointer to some future.

beyond a labyrinth
(a poem of meditation)

how is *goodsenseness* found through flawed earthly eyes
too small too infinite
exiguity belies searching each dull everywhereness

as necessary to distance myself from prognostication
as walking into cloud no chart no compass
all baggage untidily in lowland Inn
only mine eyes' own sextant to symphonize my sky
shining across meadows by lawns' living light
others dispense home wholesomeness into secret gardens

uncertainty and doubt always a-knocking doors of faith

this journey not linear but layered on chests crossed
safe-spinning idling lilies' whim
feet a-dancin', deep subterranean labyrinth

beware illusion arrest quick shadow's frightenings
sparkling keynotes through soul-darknesses
energy and essences enabling overdue excess
want not to want only your will receive
deny those suggesting there may be paths for following
focus your own place to achieve your own pace

This is a sister poem with *soul journey* although it was written a month later. Perhaps I should clarify that these poems are not arranged in the order of either conception or completion. Instead they are presented by way of narrative not as bricks in a wall but more as pebbles in a pond, not touching but connecting. As I have said, they are meant to comprise a completeness. As on a river journey each glance through port-holes provides different images but does not prevent continuity of flow.

n this Bastille Day I'm considering a lost soul locked in a sealed room of doubt, key tossed away in despondency. In the futility of *things* (to repeat GMH), is solace in devotion merely a cop-out.

I've incorporated easy rhyme except for an invented word *personalitize*. Why are the notations in song so simple yet in verse so difficult? It is possible to toil all day in the vineyard and still sweat under the shadow of the vine. Once again it is only the foot soldiers of sentence construction that I repeat, not the nouns, only one master for each ship. It is that relaxation of non or odd rhyme which brings together GMH with DMT which I have tried to embellish.

third eye of knowing
(a poem of devotion)

how may I know *Godness* not knowing myself
where lost as I am may I lose all *Self*

dry days through this journey hungry through fasting
times for words of worry nor feeling nor sensing
some night-times treading door-mats welcoming strangers
a gong calling supper a bell ringing prayers

eschew expecting ecstasy or bliss
simply enjoy contentment accepting every kiss

each soul resting as particle of spirit
powers of healing flow
where shadows of goodness flit

this is not round-race four-minute smiling
but marathon nineteen miles hour upon hour-glass glowering

nor by lee-shore crew beached ketch capsize
washed up into shallows of personalitize
waters of life retaining essence of fountains
as temple built-form melds blood-stains from saints

seed thoughts from yesterday touchstones for today
how hollowly their cry *I will repay* loses all resonance

This subtitle refers to Titian's master work, reflecting that in St John's Gospel Chapter 20 v17 the physical is not permitted whereas by v28 the spirit has no need to touch : faith being all. Its relevance now on this 60th Anniversary of the D-Day Landings is that those enduring their Blitz endeavoured that that painting did not leave London. Churchill compromised as it rested in a cave in Wales so that *not a picture shall leave these islands* as was his dictat.

rovidence provides ideas for poetry: they are all around us. In this case a dear friend Jagdish Morjaria sent me a copy of *Soul Power* by Nikki de Carteret and so this poem is for him and her: my poem to soul-consciousness. I am concerned here (as in my previous poem) with the concept of *Self*.

Through Ms de Carteret I combine Wordsworth's *trailing clouds of glory do we come* with her notion that spun within those clouds we carry our own unique spiritual DNA which it is our function to unravel. This is not pre-destination; it is the garnering of harvests. The central line concerns splitting the atom : something I suggest (living as I do too close to Aldermaston) with which others should not have trifled.

soul journey
(noll me tangere)

entering loving peace through faith
sensing spright in silence
suspending doubt releasing belief

centering on candled eye on my morrow on rising
bloom blossom bewary of priests waving sheaves
circadian clocks ticking ubiquitous rhythms

through this entirety of living forms
tiny dots specks of dust just grains of sand
mouths rejoicing from full hearts

at atom touch each *Self* implodes

where rests spiritual power whilst souls breathe
core consciousness in this disembodiment of style moderne
outer realities reflect inner responsibilities

accidents to trauma do not facilitate contemplation
nor any comprehension of pace mobility direction thrust
more wisely follow labour through ectopia

soul journey is not accomplished by tabling interrogatories
examining documents merely delays embarkation
those by roadsides accepting place may not realise their route

I have been confused for some time with make-over programmes on the Box which concentrating on built form seem to ignore vegetables, place flowers in a secondary position and give only nodding approval to an occasional tree. At this rate there will be next to no back garden but just another carbuncle to the house itself: maybe a rectangular lawn with tight herbaceous border and a few shrubs at the end to hide the neighbour's monstrosity.

ueuing at the Chelsea Flower Show in May 2004 is the causation of this piece because regrettably this has permeated the RHS. There was not one structure (for that is what they be) that I would move into Kintbury. So this is a personal poem about our garden and how I see it (which is not necessarily the same as it looks).

I've dug myself back to Gertrude (Bumps) Jekyll and her lad, Ned, matters of black and white. I came across *Terraventing* in progress at Penshurst Place in East Sussex on the 2004 Kintbury Horticultural charabanc trip. One of the pleasures of this later part of my life has been drawn from visiting gardens and collecting more of what I want but scarcely need.

looking through lawns
(of mortality)

placement of plants reflecting subconsciousness I will perceive
through natural forms into their kernel form their ka
rhythms of seasoning de-structuring ripe chopping boards
cooking and flower arranging leave weeds no hiding place

frolicking green-garnering paths

whether burning flash-fire or slowly roasting spit
commencing with blue print begin colouring
consuming cakes and ales in wildness to euphoria
casting earth-seeds on ground from which all harvests spring

lucubrate through penumbra

I stand that aged tree with ground firm trod from sod
my roots compacted with my leaves curled up through brown
I wait cultivated head-gardener prescribing Terraventing
my psychic saturates each watering-hole

foresting solicitude

seek out peaceable souls meditating mounds in grass
pull down arbours of doubts to let sufficiency run waste
accept serenity as only time replaces change
seek guidance as moon with stars splice through your space

Through these poems I've experienced my journey and reached my doorway. How I proceed further once I've pushed it ajar, entering through lobby into passageways towards waiting rooms in that house of many mansions must wait for this present. Perhaps the point may be to catch a glimpse of a transformed force in those spaces for some future. Sir John Denham's lines:

>to the same end men several paths may tread
>and many doors into one temple lead

encompass my philosophy.

Remembering my mother has been rendered more acute by the passing almost to the year of my mother-in-law Ruby through her doorway. I place here the reference to that which was GMH's favourite of his own poems. And I repeat the central phrase.

This, for Ruby, is the last to be written and I believe fittingly closes the sequence, although I have discarded three to make the collection and introduce on this, St Luke's Day, her burial, another invented word *godinus*. The goddess *Tchesert* is a symbol of purification, as plunging into a pool in a temple is just another doorway, possibly into out of body experiences not drug induced but found simply through meditation and contemplation. Maybe *godinus* appears only as *Self* disappears.

doorway
(of Tchesert)

such points of journeys showing doors
one's closed afront to push ajar or walk afar
maybe some gate to city walls unseen
in mist and damp and swirling fog or shade
tonight revealing courtyard washed soft moonshine
tomorrow opening *gardens of reeds* endlessly extending

passing through renewing all challenges denying all fear
no need to visit every room explore each corridor
mansions waxed too refined for assiduity

to make this your door to choice enter your proscribed text

look down upon your body lying still as straight
watch your brain develop *godinus* create your mind
as ghosts suggest holy souls to lifefulness
reach for that sanctuary's salonard feel his *Windhover* pass
pass through its needle-eye to blinding azure brightenings

so slowly breathe past this last sip of lip
to Samuel Palmer twilight
half dreaming summers of englishness
experiencing lifetime in all eternity's enigmas

Perhaps the world, myself, the Church, the *Word* itself are all imperfect to a purpose. A struggle to explain contradictions and absurdities in a Biblical text may be otiose. They may only serve to reflect the perfection of the *One* which all may seek but few will gain: *bewilderment* indeed. Seeking an awareness of an holistic overview I discover that the enforced agnosticism of my earlier years has become varnished by a rationalism which has painted me as mystic.

cotus (Johannes Duns) alias the *Subtle Doctor* was the mentor of GMH and their concern with *thisness* propels this poem. It is a collection of thoughts: candles of uneven height and light pricked on needles of self-consciousness.

To write in an inclusive form is difficult as much of the mystical is excluded from daytime's experience. I use *Ha Shem* as The Name and take the *principle of duty* from David Selbourne. I'm touching upon the custom of changing a person's name to reflect achievements or as a pre-requisite that conditions will change, get better. *inscape* is another GMH word being *the shape of a thing*, perhaps I would add, its *truth*. *Les Sylphides* is the ballet renamed by Diaghilev (creating new from old).

bewilderment
(Ha Shem)

part away those processes' creation
translating
body's no more of world's dimension
insignificance
hold love through strength's humility

I've probed myself to seek out ethical minorities
so many times *Les Syphides* hurled by rocks

apophatic or kataphic
chosing mystic's journey by undertaking toil
dazzling through darknesses

this *inscapes* my soul
joyness of art of beauty musicality of love
morality face forward lifetimes discesitudes

my principle of duty in my morphic field
incarnate through avatars
kenosis at her welling completing fulfillness
delimit false aspirations fend fruits from error
determine ridiculous bounds of self-delusion
through *thisness* feel soft cushion full repose non-energize

At quietus only the person is responsible; hiding in teams, skulking behind families, mixing it at work provides only temporary cover from the *Beast of Responsibility*. I wonder whether my end-days will be a capricious scherzo of prefixes; a surrender to the sex-appeal of feminine endings. As no one knows when or where *the end* will be it is cautious to consider not only tidying up but also whether there remains time to do that which is undone and (more importantly) to undo that which has been done wrongly, hastily or thoughtlessly.

his poem flows out of confusion: an admixture of seemingly endless days of Athenian Olympics, arranging Dad's 90th birthday in Newcastle and unravelling August Bank Holiday at the Edinburgh International Festival.

My penultimate poem and thus *caudal*, one before the end, the sub-title holding the *very word*. This is for John whom I have already mentioned but who continues to provide invaluable kindnesses. There is linkage running through the first word in each line as our lives have been inter-linked for over 50 years. It is meant to be full of hope and thanks. I believe it's the hope of immortality not as some sort of reward or avoidance of punishment but as continuance of a mortal search through worship.

caudal clause
(*ipsissima verba*)

each blackened shield fired glizzening glass
all reddened blazonry set shivering silver

each beard close shaved head oiled fresh quince
white robes uncertain round castle's chalk walled keep

each cell to contemplation humming wafts from praise
nor damp nor stench pure pouring warmth from scent

each well turns crystal sparkle through clear sunshine rise
dark cloaks of church surmount unholy battlements

all day through throb and heave blank energies of prayer
to Saints who step unevenly across unsettling skies

all hands peel off their roaring forties rough clock's deck
to echo dates as *Erewhon* while time freeze frame

nor through implexuous times sharp spears of vaticide
to strip off verdure to emaciate to bleed
nor gnashing teeth with oil lamps smokey dim
to entertain above must balance out unequal scales beneath
dark unbeknownst untynged undyed and unaneled
white rose to flesh each cadaver windless in faint

each soul alone accountable transparent in expectancy

It should be obvious by now that I use techniques naturally which I have not been taught but recognize through their useage, for example, (as to pick some peas):
> *paronomasia*, a play on the sounds of words
> *ploce*, word-play of puns, repeating key words
> *polyptoton*, using words in different forms

Another favourite is *antimetabole* where the same words or concepts are repeated but inversely.

arnishing and over-painting may have obscured some of these verses: I make no apology: an idea is worked upon to provide something original, perhaps unique. If that makes some lines difficult then consider reading in a garden suffuse with flowers, sit on a bench for a few minutes, pause to consider the borders laid in lines, rows, some with uneven edges, untidy endings. Gardeners and Poets face similar exercises.

Nineteen recurs throughout my work. It forms the framework of *Dossiers Secrets* where I explain it in the *Argument* as the lunar cycle. This underlines that continuity which I consider essential to an appreciation of my writing. A disciplined handling of this relationship between form and content is that which creates an individual poem and, in my opinion, if it is *a bit peculiar* then – so much the better.

Nineteen
(a poem of non-uniformity)

Oh! that we could all be changed
in such twinkling to new gowns or crowns
winding narrow bell chimed valleys to meditate new lives
clouds thinly gossamer purpling over mountains

at evening shade recounting learnings from each day
mellifluous readings from saints living ne'er dead
warmth firelight sprinkling sparkling logs

constancy of peace makes mockery to promises for change
so little needing quence some craving heart

discovering Damascene moment

by light touch of prayer candles of faith ignite
terrors of obsessive *Evil One* subsume to parody in paradise

numbering among believers including those who doubt or pale
questioning does not spring answers nor assurance
only relevance of texts heart quoted releasing doubt

turning my cape's hood inside out to breathe
full morning's freshness in this peppermint of daze
knowing a life lived lone as only half a life
fulfilled through prayer this briefest sigh sings *Oh*!

My aim has been to write in the highest of style: to compose a complete collection, a circle of 19 of those standing stones, *un oeuvre*. Each to be explored individually with the whole presenting an experience. These comprise my lament: another *Waste Land*, a century after Eliot. This taken time to turn over the corners of carpets and become concerned at that which others have swept beneath embraces permanence because it is often only a one night stand in this world of verse: too many stand up comics for my taste.

Year's anniversary of her death I close this chapter. For continuity I've introduced capitals to head the prose notes. I've taken these from the 23 letters of the Classical Roman alphabet which appear only as Capitals but omitting X and Z.

A major doubt remains as to whether these notes add anything useful to a reader. Some suggest poems should stand and speak for themselves. This is perhaps another interesting fallacy. Poets publish poems during their lifetime. They are not permitted annotation or comment. They die. Suddenly some third hand appears to explanate (I think a good word) their work. Is it not preferable for the Poet to add some *poetic notes* (perhaps extending that odd notion of *poetic licence*).

I have tilled, I fear, a patch of dead earth but now can look across my own water-meadows. It has come to me from an August 2004 Prom, Bach's Mass in B minor.

He, in his sixties, sifted through his work, tossed it in the air and watched it fall together in that wonderful *syncopacity* of sound. No giving in or up for him and none for me. I am spurred on to continue, to explore new frontiers, to experiment further with my work throughout my *19 Liners* and the Tree Alphabet (too long in silent repose). Stop being niggled: rise above criticism, let it fall away as raindrops. As if stepping out of a shower, refreshed, not only the body's surface but its whole internal including the intestines of mind were to be cleansed; leave behind the *Psycho*.

There may also be adverse comment concerning these poems being too personal. I do not resile from that: it is outwith the personal that communication springs. But I do emphasise that these are all by way of experimentation from individual pieces into a more complex whole. I am pleased to note common threads coming together in the tapestry; especially as to the *journey of the soul* and as to that I have endeavoured to elaborate (maybe sidestep) pejorative noises such as *God and that ilk*.

I hope that all these 19 pieces may be for me as poignantly retrospective as Richard Georg Straus *Vier Letzte Lieder*, his *Four Last Songs*, not attributable to any religious sect nor political movement but beginning my singing my song to this soil of England in which I hope you all may join as chorus.

                                                              Kintbury 26 December 2004

in memory of
my late mother
Christina
25 December 1914 to 23 October 2003

ramener à la route

Part Two

The Lord Jesus Christ

**five
small
loaves**

for my Father
27 viii 1914 to 12 iv 2006
memento mori

Contents

Seven Sonnets of Use & Abuse   53
    half corona of Bible Women
    (2003)

Praises   63
    psalter of seven penitential psalms
    (2004)

Ruth   73
    Novella in Verse
    (2002)

Canticles   83
    reciting Song of Songs
    (2006)

Revelation   93
    seven prayer-poems to emanation
    (2006)

St Michael's and All Angels at Enborne

Seven Sonnets of Use & Abuse
half corona of Bible Women

Ruth
Esther
Rahab
Queen of Sheba
A Woman of Samaria
Martha
Magdalene

These are from my unpublished *Songs of Insouciance* and were written especially for Valeria some years ago

A corona is 14 sonnets where the end line of the first is first of the second enjoining some link or enjoying some continuance. Here, instead of that strictness, there is a musical variation. Also the first, middle and last lines carry a similar note: liberal interpretation of I Kings 10 v 2 and 2 Chronicles 9 v 2.

The idea is to open up each story into a greater whole, linked not by obvious themes of duty and service but by a sense of sorrow which pervades throughout. It is dedicated to the vast amount of daily work that women do: men occupy a fantasy of their own, working out night and day. These poems consider the misuse of the female form.

This half Corona is arranged as Ruth and the Magdela as Maidservants, Esther and Martha as Worker-bees, Rahab and a Woman of Samaria waiting-women everywhere, with the Queen of Sheba as herself but all going about their routine business. Writing in this 2003 Iraqi war, what else would Esther see and feel? Amazement at material change but astonishment at poverty of progress in thought and morality: decisions still decided at point of a dagger.

Ruth

bible in miniature

Communing with him wholeness of her heart
       flowing together to goodness
       with wheat & oil & wine
       hearts beating his watered fields
       searing souls of satiate priests
Climbing above those barren lands
Homing to Naomi's own land

Beautiful to see and lovely to her touch
       ageing of beauty falling as leaves
       complexions wasting as waves
       her sacrifice of place of sanctuary
       each day another threshing-floor
Such sorrows as soul endures as flesh submits
Following faces through this greatness of feasts

Esther

timeless plea for racial tolerance

      another great feast following
His naked Vasti shamed through Xerxes' lust
Escapes her world of dreaming nightmares
      as those with youth dance round those old
      as mourning breaks off hope or joy
Mordecai sitting Gate of Judgement by his seat
Running ear to eye Corridors of Power

      Esther easing herself into service
Into his yoke into apprenticeship
      purpose gave her patience
      courage gave her calm
No less than death restructures boundaries
Through lovingkindness through an everlasting love
      distilling her time for words not works

Rahab

thin red line

Here squats a time for works not words
No man knows labour well as women
         & all her lovers shrink forsaken
How many men survive through cowardice
Their spouse sigh silent lacking evidence
         & promise swells to prophecy
Woman always shall encompass Man

Until His law is scribed upon their hearts
This bruise of disbelief this gripe
Scatters a flock to spoil to waste
         knowing faith without works is frail
         holding kin's hand to deal kindly
Vines on mountains grapes on hills
Her guide for travellers through her antique land

Queen of Sheba

because "she's worth it"

Aristocratic traveller from lands Arabesque
from ossuary through Sheol to resurrection
tell-tale signs of decline to this New Age
where service has declined a new tense
        fabulous King & fairy-tale Queen
         Lion of Judah & bull-horned One
Communing wholeness of her heart

Breathless in wonder before such wisdom
      as Thomas trembling to touch
      his wealth his power his justice
Subsuming her Talent with these talents of gold
& all her store of spice of silver & of sapphire stone
& all our years are gone & where & why & how
Carrying your manly labour within my womanhood

A Woman of Samaria

in propria persona

Bearing womanly labour to your manhood
Waiting by this stone-faced flint Samaria
Resting as watcher by pitcher & by tomb
Drawing off water for washing of feet
      opening through spirit into truth
      showing compassion to travellers
Her well draws law His word springs living-water

Discard your water-pot Follow your Master
Accept through Faith my Spirit through Truth
Choose Paul Apollos Cephas or your Christ
      Renew each day whom you will serve
      always reflecting God refreshes growth
      A harvest of thought brings breakfasts of wisdom
Wiping away pain from weeping eyes

Martha

distaff side

Her eyes blind weeping lashed with pain
        unbearable sweetness into service
        perfume from her jar is balm to Him
Her duty flails by Mary's feet
        His the peach peeled with spoons
        His the wine served too soon
She lays her table for their private feast

He has no need of works knowing only love
        His glint gives off a glimpse eternity
        as this earthly tent is blown away
        an altar rises through these sands
        & spindles prick at conscience of those just
That which is cherished brings forth death to life
Standing emptied in this tomb of doubt

Magdalene

first in faith

Doubt not His tomb emptied beyond doubt
Rolling away all stones of suffering
      service entails hours of attending-on
      lot of waiting-women everywhere
Holding in my breast His hurt heart
My tears enfold damp linen to His sign
Am I one She who never uses Never

It is not necessary to be doing something to be
To be with someone is sufficiency to be
      gardener or young husbandman
As we seven meet at his feet
      fragrancing an alabaster jar
Caressing our journey through our service
Wholeness of hearts communing hearts' community

St Mary's at Hampstead Marshall

Praises

psalter
of seven penitential psalms
being
another half corona

The penitential psalms are 6, 32, 38, 51, 102, 130 & 143 As 32 is a didactic poem, all of my 7 sonnets are in two parts, the first as continuing commentary on the theme "penetential", the latter concerning that particular psalm. As the headings to individual psalms are integral, I've separated the first and final lines, leaving those 2 parts as 6 lines each.

Placed in the context of my own work, this *Psalter* is a continuation of the *prayer-poems* which form the *Coda* to *Nocturne* because prayer cannot be over-stated. It comprises one whole prayer breathed in the first person (*my*) into the third person (*your*) being some spirit of your lord, not necessarily that lord himself. It anticipates, but does not expect, response; expression being sufficiency to fulfil service.

I've put 38 before 32 because the first verse of Psalms 6 and 38 are so similar. Also, the link between 32 and 51 is verse 8 of 51 not verse 1 but I've retained 51 as central as it stands major in these 7. The 150 psalms are arranged in 5 groups (maybe to reflect the *Pentateuch*) and as each group closes with a doxology, so there is such in lines 86 to 91, perhaps an *amen*.

Psalm 6 : *prayer of supplication*

sing psalms as prayer-poems sung as song

receive me in my position penitential
reverently draw off all sheets of doubt
reveal in doubling beauty of balance
embrace essence into possession
enter into an existence of completeness
entreat as one to one total oneness

how long to endure rebukes in anger
as my eye fades as my breath fails
weary with groaning my sore vexed soul
swimming in night-watering tears
chastened by death of remembrancing
receive my prayer accept my pleading voice

lord let not discipline cool your disciple in anger

Psalm 38 : *prayer of remembrance*

neither chastening in hot displeasure lord

in penitence undertake voluntary repentence
as Augustine pinned prayers to his dying cells
washed with his labiate in sombre full black suit
hold this reverential tome against blood-money
as that price has been paid and redeemed
let complaints from those devout but sick desist

all lengths of my desiring lie within your eyes
while deaf and dumb to arrows of adversity
to brevity to vanities of life's
snares through deceits of disease
do not reject me as some hideous corpse
but hasten your steps as my foot sideways slips

rendering myself ready in sorrow for blessing

Psalm 32 : *prayer of admission*

for blessed is that One who steadies sorrows

make this as now my book for praising
contemplating all of past this present and all futures
full prophetic hope where all is as forgiveness
as each song sounding notes of truth
to my Becoming One offering individual lament
of adoration into trust with confidence confess

not mule nor horse-like bit and bridle
but understanding your mastery advances
all those faithful praying to your blessings
as parched hearts as stubble rains rejoice
from summer's drought until his haywain
becomes my hiding place my harbour refuge

rejoice be glad and shout with honest hearts for joy

Psalm 51 : *prayer of contrition*

joy in rejoicing opening to gladness loving hearts

in a penitentiary of my choosing learning prayer
moods move expressing faiths to festive celebration
not doomed to bitterness solemnity nor sorrow
let those who love your name rejoice set free
for by your mercy are you feared
before each morning's watch my soul must fly

as these bones crushed begin their dance delight
need's cleansed by contrition no longer decrement
accept atonement in full penitence
no longer far off from your face of grace
all secret wisdoms teach through standing stones
purged hyssop shining whiter than mountain snow

let praise rise through prayer not sacrifice

Psalm 102 : *prayer of affliction*

hear my life-cry of prayer not death-cry from bones

my faith pennaceous as quill-feather
adopts these psalms as comfort as inspiration
following them to their source of guidance
obeying their commands entreating warnings
death becomes no longer my supreme enemy
finality remains ultimate only if lacking of eternity

cast aside ashes for bread withered as grass
my days shadow a desert-owl sweeping on waste
consumed my bones smoke smouldering hearth
reviling wrath of those destitute so remember me
from heights of strength of your sanctuary
hear this captive sighing for dwelling in your presence

from foundation of this earth hear my plea

Psalm 130 : *prayer of hope*

my plea accept through heaven's extremity

light plucking harp-strings of my heart
with harpsichord dulcimer and zither
all psalms rise to you addressed by assembled
throngs in songs shrill ascent from *de profundis*
to deliver me from bloodguiltiness
to refresh my face with dews of morning

each morning I watch and wait for manna of birdsong
marking each phase of your moon with new hope
that your record of my wrongfulness may be undone
that in my release you will be revered
as that watchman *What of the Night* crying
watch and prayfully wait for dawning's plenteous fruit

by supplications your servant subsumes your answer

Psalm 143 : *prayer of entrity*

your righteousness answers all your servant's desiring

in this doxology presenting hymn in praise of he
who searches souls for brevity enhonouring *Trinity*
lamenting pain for grief of darkness into shame
no unbelief lies in one complaining no
presenting this lament transforming miracles of praise
my heart skips desperate as my soul gasps faint

dwelling in darkness am I desolate as those departed
or meditating upon your handiwork
will your muse infuse my hand outreached
as cold water to this thirsty pours forth good news
so my spirit shall not fail your hiding-place
you quickening my troubled soul to equilibrium

singing this song as poem pure prayer-psalm

                                              hallelujah

St Lawrence's at West Woodhay

… **Ruth**

Novella in Verse

I've great respect for verse-play, especially reflecting the structure of relationships. Contained within these Old Testament stories there remains much truth and guidance. Listening to the Bible as a child, reading it for myself later and studying Commentaries and the rest, it is not possible to acknowledge all the sources used. However, it was on finding *The Anchor Bible* that I formed the idea of writing this Poem and I thank Edward F Campbell Jnr for his translation of *Ruth* (Doubleday, New York 1997) which suggested to me this *verse-play*.

The concept of this Poem came to me while staying at the *Mena House Oberoi* in Cairo and its structure on the Terrace of the *Old Cataract Hotel* in Aswan. I wrote the First Draft on the River Nile lazing down to Luxor over Easter Weekend 2002. Much of my work springs from Easter's spirit of refreshment, renewing faith.

One

Naomi
My lads my husband
Lie dead in Moab
For all your loving-kindness to myself
And to my dead I release you to your own
Go find cold comfort of house of husband
Yahweh flow back those waters dried out in tears
But Ruth refused her

Ruth
With you return we to your land your people

Naomi
Turn your back on me
I am dried to barren
Too old to husband
Too sad to hope
If sons I could bear
How long would you wait
Not till they harvested
By then you barren too
Thus life restrains
Thus my lord proclaims
Freshing Naomi's cheek leaving Orpah's kiss
She returning to her birth place
Resting ground of every lost family

Two

Naomi
Follow your sister-in-law to her people
Back to her known Lord
But Ruth refused her
Ruth clinging mother-in-law's apron strings

Ruth
Don't press me to leave
Abandon you
Where you lodge I lodge
Your own folk as my folk
Your lord my lord
Where buried you lie
There buried lie aye
Whatever our lord does to you
Does to me also else I die

Argument superfluous to these new sisters
Handed in hand to Jerusalem's gates
From plateau of Moab
From death of her husband
From twin tears for dead sons
From all famine and sorrow
From waiting and watching
From their ten years in service
Both steadfastly minded tread forth

Three

City excited cries:

Is it Naomi?

Naomi
Don't call me sweet one
Dub me as bitter one
Yahweh has emptied me
Sadday has filled me
Souring his bitterness
I cannot be sweet one
Now my lord's condemned me

Their work not being done is still to do
Their battle has become their life's campaign
This is beginning of new times for ripening Ruth
This towards commencement of barley harvesting
Full formed in an ear mature not yet full ripe

Ruth
I go to his fields
To glean his barley
To gain his eye

As that lad with five small barley loaves
So Ruth presents her new work to her new lord

Four

So *Yahweh* guided Ruth to fields of Boaz
Kinsman to widow Naomi's husband

Boaz
Do not glean another field
Glean for me with many maidens
Gather my sheaves after my reapers
No young man attend you
Everyone protect you
When you thirst drink from these cups
Stay by my fireside rest in my wings

Ruth
Why show me such grace
Why open your place

Boaz
All you sacrificed for Naomi
Shall be repayed you
All you've abandoned
Shall be fulfilled

For this reason men shall leave mothers
Life staggers between pain and pleasures
Children idiotic play old mad fools
Those heathen those wicked those buffooned

Five

After his twilight spent winnowing
Enjoying flowing of fine wines rich spices
Boaz at rest in granary's darkness
At his feet anointing his princess

Boaz
Draw down by my side
Partake of my wine dip in your bread
Show me your kindness

Ruth
I am Ruth your maidservant
My redeemer fold under your wings

Boaz
Another redeemer nearer than I
If he fails then redeemer am I
For shunning those younger
Those richer those poorer
All you ask shall I give you
All you say shall you have
You have made me your hesed
Lie quiet quite still til morning
Leave me by this threshing floor
Take all measures wrapped around you
With me pray this night for our morrow

Six

Boaz redeemer by city gate
And nearer redeemer meet
Selecting ten elders passing by
With public eyes with time to sit or stare

Boaz
Naomi offers for sale her part of her field
one party has first choice but afterwards just me
ploughing straight from Elimeleck's fields

But near redeemer pauses
Purchasing assumes responsibility
Not just Naomi's blood
Although her field may income yield
But cost of Ruth her fruits and all their rights
May mean to dispossess his own
This much this other could not justify
This nameless one could not redeem and thus her cup
Passed back to Boaz who shoed onwards passed

Boaz
I take this field Naomi my new wife Ruth
To establish in their name those dead
So that from his brethren from this assembly
His name is not cut off but lives through offspring
All those round that gate bore witness one and all

Seven

To Ruth and Boaz their son born Obed
To Naomi as nursemaid her grandson
Who fathering Jesse fathered David

There is a point beyond which faith cannot
Endure else resting on some others' sacrifice

Placing themselves at mercy of Boaz
Changing Ruth's threshing floor restfulness
For restlessness of Boaz by an opened gate
That nameless one is law's impediment
Faith overcomes to reach a state of grace
Law resolves nothing on pathways to faith

Naomi
Now I'm your sweet one
Completely fulfilled
My sentence annulled
Bitterness for no one

Ruth gleaning through harvests of barley of wheat
In safe fields of Boaz kinsman and friend
His hesed to those living along with those dead
Ruth's cries all answered Naomi's fulfilled
Mid alien corn sojourning in peace
Redeemer restored nourished with love

St Swithun's at Coombe

Canticles

reciting
Song of Songs

Song of Songs (omitting the first 4 and the closing 10 verses) comprises 5 distinct poems as:
    1.5 to 2.7
    8.8 to 3.5
    6.6 to 5.1
    2.2 to 6.3
    4.4 to 8.4

Eve's *Song* sung in her Garden, later by Sheba's Queen to Solomon where passion curves a fertile crescent amongst those most beautiful of all created. I'm reflecting upon that most enduring of English creations: *the garden*, moving Eden to my own Kennet Valley and so (in reality) who can say my Lord does not walk here not only at eventide but ever in his given light; walk in and enjoy.

My 5 central poems are in 2 parts, first concerning each particular *Song*, second (following a central line) comprising a continuous Eco Poem. I've added an Opening and Closing piece to make these 7 poems which originated at the South Bank on my daughter Daisy's 21st birthday while experiencing Salvadore Dali's exhibition and his 12 images from the *Song of Solomon*. My chosen accompanying music is an English voice, Ralph Vaughan Williams' *Toward the Unknown Region*.

Opening

towards those unknown regions where so long before
planted and tended to eastwards of Eden
where passions cool only with lightness through eventide

singing in this garden of delights first sanctuary
soliliquies of ritual blessings to rejuvenate this spirit
is wisdom simply sensing through loving real love

I am kneaded into clay which is your flesh
I am clothed in your wrappings of virtue
I am tasting sweet waters abrading my senses

while poems of wonderment belie me

may this song touch you as kisses on your mouth
for love is longerlasting than wineing or desiring
and allegory flits too easily amongst mysteries

as his word is hewn in woods of histories
remembering those toiling vineyards to dewtimes of mornings
untroubled unsullied preparing for everlasting peace

I step down into his ford which crosses his river
I look to his bridge between heaven and earth
I am moved to worshippers watering to refreshment

First Song

hear my soliloquy in these vineyards of sweet cicely
with kissings of wines scentings of spikenard
reclining clusters of camphire bowerings of desirings

rose and lily rest by my valley by goddess of fields
of spirits of flowers as smiles flow fellowships
drawing aside soft folds of dreaming into lovingness

leaving me feasting softness of tender hart or roe
chasing chimera through mountains of myrrh
as winter's rain drives summer's scent from fox-free vine

banish darkness of desert tents to moonbeams of beauties

walking in this garden this evening walking
with my lord his fellowship his understanding
heart who hears my prayer before it leaves my heart

how easy in this garden is to fall in love
in love how easily are gardeners' delights
designed to reproduce through love's uneasy arts

unhappy weeds their profligating seeds
addressing in expectancy in volts which vitalise
reflecting in my garden's face all that love reflects

Second Song

rise from love's nest where soul's embrace conceives
to fields of hinds on wakening startling gazelle
through verse through song to passionate lovingness

this season of songs' gladstone as rains are reserved
song-birds trill to cooing of turtle-doves' refrain
enfreshing sustainment through sweetness of tasting

in greenness rest beddings of peacefulness
to sixteenth summertime whilst walnuts frunctify
as apples crushed to cydre vaporise to fragrances

voice sweet your comely face to improvise to please

wandering through gardens find treasure troves of wondering
of cultural concerns of personal perhaps sophistic sights
many metaphors of gardens rest inert

but as to ground elder always respect tenacity
experience through husbandry life's whole experience
enjoy as theatre this gardenworld of dream delights

replace in space some urns some temples or removes
erect more follies than prudent sanity permits
in riversrun drain pools of doubt from drought

Third Song

from haunts of lions mountains of leopards
emerging swirling smoke from wildernesses
vibrant chariots of wood of silver of gold thigh-strapped

warriors their mighty shields clanking from night's fear
awakening to breaths of spices of fruits of saffron
cinnamon incense aloes full frankincense

with purples covering maids' chasteness as bridegroom
warms to bride with honeycomb fresh splashed spiced wine
anointing pleasures anew as new day breaks full fair

spared sheep from shearing goats from grazing eased

come into this garden feast its festive fruits
feed from spatial arts blessings of nature's bounties
reflect below this boundless sky flora and fauna

shrub off this shrubbery emerge from maze of ways
respect this gardenist his fulfilment herb and spice
fruit and flower impatient waiting through expectancy

as so many sons from Adam with daughters full supportive
to (in his wisdom) Solomon overcome with concubines
their winsome smiles at tinkerings of spade of fork of trowel

Fourth Song

sleep awakens heart's restlessness in trilling
of doves on dewdrops of nightfulness as my touch
reaches your doorway your pleasance unlocks

sweet-scenting parterre for flowering into abundance
now opening from sleeping to your wakening voice
to heights of passions adhering your enabling breath

standing tall as cedars rising pillars of gold
your raven curls bushy and black your eyes
washing rivers of milk feasting your honeycomb

I am now become as my belovéd am I

once blanched midsummer heat turns autumnal warmth
learn at least for one year some flowering of knowing
some gracefulness in indifferent face of nature

gardens are performances of motion silently effective
subversive not undecided over catalogues and lists
knowing it's not half an afternoon but every day

to nightfall when with hampers packed away
with all there is remains to entertain to play
to remembrancing of solicitude in solitude

Fifth Song

as fair as my moon is my morning's brightness
as my love my dove my flowering vinolent
arising to renewal to new year's growing to birthing

everywhere offering tenderness to harvesting
in every cycle heaps of wheat tower as ivory safely
homed by your galleries where play purpled princesses

I have shaken dates off from your highest palm
I pluck grapes and figs in your abundant balm
I sing your delights through arms of love's psalm

expressing in harmony humanity's express

how much is needful of remembrance in this garden
a well-disciplined and tender soul in fellowship
transcendently rapping mysteries of divine loving

an excellence in intimacy holding some mystical
some tender spirit after day's work replete
all that remains is fellowship with whosoever remains

I find a small churchyard pressed by a vineyard
I blink at an army with banners alarming
I voice as amenuensis an all persuasive persona

Closing

as allusion as symbol as love-poem as longings
as frustrations appealing from ancient to modern desirings
leave dark tents of dwellers in deserts to tend flocks

on well-watering pastures casting off your veil ceasing on
wanderings providing blushings of exotic luxuries
enhancing my couch with gazelles in clefts of hillsides

where lilies gather showing banners of joy where orchards
bloom as dancers' pirouette spin souls reveal
in dreams are lives devised in greensward's lyric imagery

where love is open everywhere is love

plants blossoming as poems too beautiful to prune
arousing in spring this better this lovelier this greener space
fairest place for spices lubricants for purifants

where mystics reach out beyond proscribed divides
lovers must always crave to carve from flesh
their words of beauty poetry whole imagined worlds

and so to this ending of no ending
retaining on closing remnants of loving
in these mysteries harbour dreams in your own arbour

St Michael's at Inkpen

Revelation

being
seven prayer-poems to emanation

overture
prescience
parousia
melange
apocalypse
millennium
finalé

presented in my *19 liner* format

There are two strands inter-twined through this poem, 7 visions from the Revelation of St John the Divine and 7 images from the 7 stages of Creation, thus bringing *Genesis* and *Revelation*, the first and last books of the *Holy Bible,* together as one. They comprise a series of dream sequences moving in and out of themselves as broken yet recurring fragments until, through varied repetitions, they attain almost some realness.

A conundrum with any *Revelation* is that once all is revealed there remains no more; which may explain an emphasis upon imminence. I regard this as being one wholeness not some sum of parts, perhaps it is *peripeteia*.

overture

husbanding things on earth uplifting things to heaven

here testifies my message for prophetic minorities
for artists for visionaries for messengers
reflecting *Daniel's* script
towards some ultimate some universal kingdom
pointing towards an eschatological time to come

this cosmos marred by struggling powers non-compatable
identifying transcendence from merely spatial
never sealing up images of prophesy
but letting letters pass hand's palm to heart's ease

bring me my benediction into my garden of evening prayer

as for me *Genesis* and *Revelation* are two clasps
or buckles on my belt my girdle to beautiful divine
singing highest register never muted tones
sensing visions always revealing dreams

read me not progressively but recapitulatary
concentrating this polyvalence as poetry first
counting out in numbers several secrets of seven
in this eternal vision for evermore good over evil
for this day forever foretells wholeness of histories

prescience

an infallible foreknowledge

continuing an eternal commission to write to record
as seen revealed never fully understood
as incomprehensible drawings on walls of caves
firelight flickering echoing unseen voices

in this encampment of those sanctified saved
distractions of demonic netherworlds
being in spirit ascend this door opening heavenly
beings their seas of glass centre realities
in cosmos transformed from transitory into permanence

an end to lament apology error dirge and woe

I am less than one grain of sand washed eternal
oceans of Lord's hopes and promises one grain
held between bricks in this new this holy city
in my reality of hope is my foundation for future
not so far revealed *things* and so as ever feared

from salvation's mountain regret past wildernesses
let all acclaim an end to evilness
temples of stones recast as shrines to saints'
worldlessness as nations powerless fade to less

parousia

bread of presence

breaking seals for soul's salvation
handling uncertainties over-coming wishful-thinkingness
never compromise fellowship's earnestness of worshipping
avoid those countless multitudes who may not count
in facing evil eliminate through prayer its power's prowess

kneel in prayer revere to martyr's flowing bloods
to cleanse unclean as scriptures stress their sacred text
as hellish hades exonerates every heathen misandry
fulfilling subtifuge in shadowy shapes of sorrowing

warfare in heaven reflects no peace on earth

as candles' frailties flicker mysteries into failing gasps
so exegetes intoning snuffburn their fingers
presenting persecutions with immanent destruction
respond to flames my mantra prayer chant

here is comfort here is hope's deliverance
scattering through seven beatitudes across assembled angels
anguish and abominations dashed to desolation

there is no end to days only day's ending where
quietly composed quiescence lies reposed

melange

olla-podrida

wave over wave image upon image
overflowing impressions of movements of colour
of gold of silver of brass and all of iron
souls marbling thysene wood in rainbows of emeralds

I see a crystal sea of glass as cups of pearls
jasper and sardine stones harps and vials
trumpets and girdles censers upon incense
robed in pure white linen lined purple silk with scarlet
glory showing honour wisdom shining blessing

and all measuring and balancing wheat over barley

one opening another door positioning corridors of mirrors
reflecting passages of time's eventual tread
feasting off this tree of life alive for evermore
now crowned with pomegranates lighting candles

these stories continue through coincidence
as others collecting chalcedony sapphire or sardius
sardonzy or chyrolite with beryl topaz even jacinth
I make those twelve with amethyst with chryropasus
so now I rest my eyes through sleeps of scents

apocalypse

visible things transitory eternal things invisible

as riders as chariots splice to spin outriders
(conquering these brings only other conquistidors)
maybe there rests inherent always apocalyptic expectation
of divine judgement of myriads of angelic faces

as martyrs stretch through nights of wrath of woe
or flames lick and trick hours of testing
evil backhands me at my net of truth
failed hymns to praise Hail Mary's pleas of prayer
I've inventorised so much I never ever will begin again

adventuring pale on black and red on white four horsemen

unveil my future traced through my past
in present tensions disclose divine mysteries
translation of revelation is personal and private
prevents ultimate solution to human misery & suffering

let me see again sights which ancients saw
reviving new hopes in this global heeding of nature's warnings
of cataclysmic cosmic failings treading toes of past prophets
hear their din as angels weep & wail
mad blindness rushing through disaster into mayhem

millennium

mythical heaven

with thousands of silks of linen-clad figurines
tight garmented meeting and greeting each
with a kiss a touch an embrace of love
for love passes all understanding in this timeless
city mason-formed four-square citadel
lit with light from its own stones its palaces
with opened gates shunning threats of night-scape
on this high plateau cleanest air freshest water
with balming breeze fruiting recurring monthly berries

ambrosia and nectar over-flowing cup and dish

in this paradise this place full peacefulness
a sea-less landscape stretching heavenwards
all tears are wiped away as faces smile
as brides on wedding mornings outshine their maids
neither pain nor death nor sorrowings

fountains flowing for ever quenching pure waters of life
radient with righteousness with holiness
singing their messages faithful to redeeming trust
before all endings into faithfulness beyond beginnings

finalé

eternal dhama

key your future by twisting tomorrow's hand
or will it simply be more of some past but slower
skimming as pebbles to this shore's horizon those distant
figures astound rounding each receding headland
and my next until with wind onshore beached am I becalmed

all that is necessary is to remove time's play
which bars imagination's flow creative
wisdom's tide to knowledge by experience
attain one ultimate one universal state of sense

this spirit will illuminate in private prayer each single soul

here lie foolish bridesmaids dithering their groom to come
in flickering nightshades of doubts of weariness
their loving one who breathes new scents of life
who bathes their hearts with oils with essences
and cleanses all who kneel in purged belief

here is revealed that which is unknowable
matters of unsurpassed significance
there is sensing of speaking hearing only whispering words
soundings to understanding far beyond frailty's comprehension

St Mary the Virgin at Kintbury with Avington

Part Three

Paul & Apollos

19

recent

Nineteen Liners

Adam & Eve

19 recent Nineteen Liners

by Bucklebury Church   109

power of sorrow   110

impromptu in uprooted times
for a *New Sanctuary in an Old Grove*   111

authorless texts resting on sacred
or *The Book of Common Prayer*   112

incomprehensibility   113

difficulty of naming poems being orphans
for *Dr Martin Lings*   114

caravansera   115

observations upon Mount Athos
(*hearts of inscrutable silence*)   116

concepts of leaving may not always entreat loss
for *my brother's birthday*   117

Muhammed's Grave
(*detritus of death*)   118

after another prayer meeting
(*sing hallelujah*) 119

in a lived life
(*episcopus*) 120

resurrection
(*maybe fable*) 121

untitled
(*compiled from found notes*) 122

Is everything wrong
(*or is it only me*) 123

A Future
(*without a prayer*) 124

Is There
(*almost certainly there is*) 125

closure 126

This *thing* called Faith 127

by Bucklebury Church

when dreaming through your own death
be watchful not to note your own night's time
concentrate on space those reflective faces
avoid and peer outwards beyond contra positioning

I've seen them simultaneously together
joined by a river's side or posing round a figurine
which enlarging into light moves into me
propels me deeper inside its ecstasies
in waves in tremors in elasticity's release
fold upon fold silk and cotton and wool
touching my skin as her soft hand massages
worries from brows harrows from anxieties

afterwards my room littered with used clothes
unwashed glasses lingerings of old lingerie
stale perfumes spent force lost chance

and I am paralysed in sweat by fear
cowardice colours my yellowing conscience

and I notice as stigmata on a wall by a window
in dreaming your face younger beautifully divine

power of sorrow

in your given life free yourself from pastness
overcome that which others may or may not have pressed
upon your own immortal and everlasting soul's
breathing to retaining memories of regrets not forgot

become your still your own centre throughout eternity
improving brick by brick your own city state
no golden crown cast bestride gossamer seas

in acclaiming such or even just attempting such
begin new *things* endure fresh starts

invoke imprecotary psalms

spite cuts open wounds of deepest of noblest spirits
discarnate heavenly states
repaying effortlessness throughout distress
faith devours all doubts through works

my life is only one tare in a rushing flood of tears
an eye glanced away in a passageway

I need to bind together these secret threads of love
observing holy seasons into grace or favour
astride my elephant her tread springs up new grasses

impromptu in uprooted times

for *a New Sanctuary in an Old Grove*

seek sanctuary within spiritual tradition
        not inaction from drawn distance
sensing appearance in my beloved's face
        in throes of wounds to death's
opening of closed books to new openings
        prophesizing beauties of designs
presenting trophies onto cabinets of delights

where is this solace sought but unfound
        show me to my pathway for my slow
unworthy shoe to dust across sapped sands

building Divine Presence into circled sanctuaries
        of sapphire of gold precious stones
of gems inscribed with messages of holiness
reflecting serpentless Eden's garden of purities

poised in this prism nor beginning neither end
pierce mystery reveal radiance of revelation
replace formlessness with structures for worship

into sanctuary full-blooded pour out whole hearts
ease off unease anoint cleansed purpleness of peace

authorless texts resting on sacred
or *The Book of Common Prayer*

      write hand first flaming into right
to recant to burn as words scorch skin as paper thin
firing their faggots to deep breaths of faith
embracing old friends undoing new enemies

      of humbler temper throughout reigns of change
strength & weakness charm & pathos
ever compromising beneath old or new
as fanaticism infils those less reflective too responsive

there concealed in prose a lyricism of verse
    in this lectionary for those visionary
      with richest cadence ciceronian
before which doctrine and practice pass away
seeking not happiness but cessassion of sorrowing

believers stand steadfast after You liturgical formal
    from baptism toiling into communion
praying in kinship in privacy of place
muddling' mid Doubter's sword Believer's shield
what is expected flails all expectation

through liturgy preserve this unnatural text for evermore

incomprehensibility

I have wandered amongst ruins of friends' lives
I have sung of wasted nights through unrealisable dreams
I have never doubted my sincerity into thoughtlessness
I have rarely troubled an umpire as I scratched for singles

I have looked back too much over other shoulders
I have forgotten memories I should have recounted
I have faces in focus who are unrecognisable
I have presented a front of transparent effrontery

to my past I owe a debt of ingratitude
to this present I've earned almost total incomprehensibility
to our future I fear impossibility to any shape of continuity

Why do I need to regard this dark past pleasantly
Why can't I just shrug it all off as a shorn shrift
Why is it not possible to live today always in tomorrow
Why is yesterday such a weight of ashen dust of failure

How will this world be with each smoker as solitary drinker
How many pubs reforming emptied churches vacated chapels

How can I hope to endure any of this (and as to How)
How with webbed information How can knowledge ever inform

difficulty of naming poems being orphans

    for Dr Martin Lings

they are as rare today wise and holy folk
      exemplars of paradigms of basic theory
no longer lost to some hermeneutics of social form

standing in permanency of impermanence
symbolising knowledge only moonlight reflects
      he stays here this day in certainty of substance

    whosoever I shall seek shall I find
    finding may I know to love
    loving may I cease my search

    divine favour remains essential necessity

I know its secret name this sacred jewel
      guarded by dragons of doubt of gloom
watched by warriors through cloud through rain

I have woven my text from threads of cloth
      avoiding fires which flame immortal light
beating rhythms from my lord's chosen metre

    seeking my heavenly hermitage
from ferment off disorder to order of tranquillity
      philosophizing only by means of myth

caravansera

here deep in our desert our place of rest
court quartered round this spacious court
its silence swallowing sounds of sleeping guards
of camels' restless chewing of their cords uncut
knarled teeth refracting unsheathed curved blades

on its quadrangular walls at strokes of night
snatches of moon-fright noises of doom
delight of being in this new space new found place
far off from spirits of those dead rattlings of those dying

I am your mold after your face is cast
so far removed from random collisions
of cosmic rays in space of big bang's second second
I am as anti-matter to what matters most
I hold in my eye the cleft of your pathetic fallacy

are we judged upon our wholeness of life
or only upon a single paragraph perhaps a phrase
wholly out of character circumscribed by circumstance

linen left unfolded for her bridesmaid's gaze
dusts of foreign chambers placeboes in uncollected baggages

observations upon Mount Athos

(hearts of inscrutable silence)

Do we all have a *Mount Athos* in our minds
a place for straying away from *Lands of Spirits*
a paradise surrounded by Holy Mountains
Do we have to chose from living amongst those dead

Burnt by fires at cave's opening
I'm purified by suffering into cool shades
into depths of dark drippings of time's waterings
Bringing me cosmic knowledge wanderings into wisdom

I am become a slave to routine
        bound to my breadless table nightly
I am unable to escape save through thoughts
        boundless in their energy incense burning intently

When I fall upon a new cherub
I will pull its beard to assess its experience
of sensual pleasures delights into exhuberance
When I'm plucking shrubs my garden's full of fruits

Do I need to end my days amongst those only Christian
        on an island above sea mists rising valley fogs
Do I have any choice Do I care Do I really need to choose

concepts of leaving may not always entreat loss

for my brother's birthday

there have been lengthened these years so many leavings
      that there may be nought else to leave

there have been so many walkings away or from
      that there may be no one else left to leave
          or stray away from

movements of doors closing which inhere such quiescence
      that not even mice can sense
incandescence into nightscapes of undecidedness

who cares my tipple tends my pleasure tempts my poise
      may all be opened with nothing dreich
away from gluttony devouring talent into fame

attempting to formulate my mystical experience
      communicating through poetic or devotional lines
always embracing something more than metaphysical

metaphorically beating this heart into a bosom of all *things*
      irreductable as describing ineffective felicity
leaving only sprinklers splashing lawns as stumps are drawn

sitting down some back row choosing whom I will to serve
not reckoning how many bowers bowed to bind my corpus

Muhammad's Grave

(detritus of death)

I have watched and washed
    away each tear and fear
I have encountered cemeteries
    and counted tombs and dooms
I have breathed dense stench of death
    with wailing women ululating
I have glanced on mountainsides bright shrines
    of glistening brass of slow funereal rites

I have touched his corpse with this undying hand
    and felt his clay deep dug beneath his bed
I have toiled through all so many burial grounds
    to bring a lingering of camphor oils of myrth
I have examined evasive systems to eternities

I have considered various rituals of mourning
    its paradox a body's presence in absence
I have unpicked shrouds of ambiguity
    numerous pieties presenting their assurances
I have enlightened in rooms funerary candles
    in which old prophets learn to yearn to die

after another prayer meeting

(sing hallelujah)

poetry may be my way of stepping away from silence
my way of loosening out of line
whilst remaining taught

so many religions so much untruth
whatever ever represents
normative value for some prayerful few

is despair that surgery which emasculates justice
an attitude piatitude
some stance to rectitude

I begin with this counting of several falling leaves

through storms of doubt I survive without
any fatherly abode immortal unending no-placed
rejoicing always in joyance of joy's delights

rather than seeking evolution embrace revelation
libations to closer living together

Yama first mortal first mountaineer
first examiner resting under Yaruna's righteous tree

minds echoing prayer are as excretions of power

prayer calms minds absent of powerless complexities

in a lived life

    (episcopus)

      work as her own prerequisite
personally experiencing sweat as its own reward
explaining some personality deficiency
      may satisfy those of an intellectual disposition
moving into believing inside an eternal mind

which creates any impossible universe anywhere
which is useless to me not sustaining of life
which does not present a lasting hope for death
which does not preserve that invariable my own mortality

      soul eats a body's heart dried out

there are soul-mates who kick our guts out
      which mark an end of any heroic age
of chivalry good mannerisms all gone bad

study spiritual experience seek out collective
consciousness defining religious differences
set all those to that one side divisiveness

some sing moments of heightened awareness as they sway
out of bodily existence into this floating labyrinth
this broad church my space absent of methodology

resurrection

(maybe fable)

holding sight of half-moon longing for sigh of air
stillness of less than touch of scent breathlessly waiting
my third morning with prayer-psalms of nineteen pauses
      mind makes me not me mastering mind

in journeys from this world of forms preparing souls
for transcendent unity of all believings
in mind of memory of thought of need desiring
      breathe prayer's living air within day breathing

forgiveness must be foremost in my flight from fear
      prayer of heart perfection into prayer
making peace with my lord peace of man my own making

ultimate triumph is divine love in human living
treading by truth through reality into transcendence
excitements freed from religion's formulations
finding through penance pure purpose of penitence

in continuing wayfaring ignore path's tares and weeds
observe verdancy of thought countryside surround

in becoming lost only am I becoming found
foundling no more I stretch across this folded shroud

untitled

(compiled from found notes)

just enquire of those fellows harvesting hay
        beneath their long low suffering skies
enquiring patterns through deep troughs of ploughing
          watching horses wallowing each furrowing

big root Bryony heaving her coat a-shine
        seven shaded chestnut sorrel-eyed
        snorting off morning till yardarm's spun
such length of journey inveighing each and every day
        chaucerian continuum endangering simple flowers

another summer silenced for a wintertime of warmth

sloe hatching is as coldest as bleak blackthorne breaks
        harrowing in faery dancing

another couple into new pressed shirts and all washed up
        his thrush stopped singing as her shepherd died

in taverns by drying docks or hostels round mystic green
        all cough up separately their collier's lung

        in core of heart of all that's living
supreme in personality my lord director
        resides my super-soul in waiting's time

Is everything wrong

    (or is it only me)

is this devilish machine breaking down
      if it is may my faith fix it

I have watched planting throughout this garden
      tiny placements growing intricate patterns
soils obeying rain's commandments as I taste my fruits
      of labours of others uncomplaining

I am impotent once seed is sown as minute
particles of bodies impress themselves precisely

considering unobservable realms
      hypothesis non fingo
as I lie back to count her faces on my moon's beam

should there only be this mechanical vision
presuming plants projectiles & other phenomena

as evidence is shovelled on my wasting remains
may curtains of moral certainties be rent

is rationality a matter of choice or of compulsion
      so much forbid too much permit

let me release my spirit my spring of air
remaining uncertain whatever tomorrow leaves remaining

A Future

    (without a prayer)

I have leaves of His word in this wood of my life
I hold satires of saints in gasps of daze
I take inspiration from each breath he gives me breathe
I tear from myself tight bindings of self-doubt

Exhuberant with excitement in revelation
soul satisfied spirit saturate senses satiate

My Lord's message through his messengers
each day every morning and all of a night
comprehension following reading into understanding

    in eyes of desire hope springs

Crossing over waters stepping each unsteadied stone
hoping for more than either milk or honey perhaps
some oil (not in a widow's jar)
    (no balm in Gilliad)

I'm on that other side for now in time
    looking backwards into intensity
    insensitive of when or how
    deliberately askance and why

dew drops or other manna of food in uncertain supply

Is There

(almost certainly there is)

timeless things only exit through lessness of time

I am a colourblind cloud a particle of an emptied mind
I am neither always is nor never was
an inelaborate element of subjective interpretation

is good-godness a source of order or of law

truthing through plausibilities of metaphysical hypothesis
something else almost probabilistically predictable
stimulating argument to generate intelligent debate

gods of necessity need proof of their goodness
activity versus content
unalterable laws frame a forum for an unattainable

can simplicity exist in a more complex cosmology
creating awkward likelihoods of intrinsic correlations
suggesting towards purpose even value in this eternity

or is it merely for unusuallity to predict or foresee newness

it is for us to grasp to comprehend to make
intelligable this universe we've been rewarded with
through song and dance with peace and love and prayer

why on earth is this *Earth* where it is on earth

closure

if I were only one and not this sum of parts
if only I could pause pretending not to comprehend
but
into this emptiness of living I must spill hope's
enjoyment into other spheres of cognisance
yet
when presence presents an absence of prescience
am I more disparate as clouds disperse
or just more desperate as moons occlude

there may be truth in uncertainty of movement
thoughts not having enough time to reduce to writing
while words envelop themselves in complexity's density
now
I'm so completely lost I'm endangered specie

I stretch my Lord's hand he moves not a finger

there have been too many meetings of minds

so
there is nothing I can do
there is nowhere I can go

This *thing* called Faith

At the end of your day
as you pause in prayer
turn all *things* to faith

No matter your extent of knowledge
your learning
your understanding of eternal truth
your individual wisdom
whatever texts you've read
committed to your memory
translated or composed yourself
whoever you have taught
or has taught yourself
whichever tribe or custom you may share
whichever church or mission
school or discipline
may hold you in its temporary thrall

At the end of whichever is your last day
all you will have to hold you fast
is your belief in this *thing* called faith

David & Jonathan

Part Four

God is Great

CODA: *Appearances*

Appearances

It may be a truism that "attempts to harmonize these traditions have failed to persuade critics, but the testimony of the biblical witnesses to the Divine event itself is unanimous" [1]

These Appearances after my Lord's *Resurrection* taken with *Transfiguration* and *Ascension* comprise those marvels which constitute a corner-stone upon which Christianity is built: it is that which distinguishes it from other religions. Many may die for their own belief but none rise from their own dead-ness. This is different from the Lord restoring to her full life Jairus' daughter or raising Lazarus from his deadness: here he regenerates Himself, *unaided*. I put that deliberately in italics because something fundamental has occurred. Since his mortal death he re-emerges into the *Holy Spirit*: this is his gift, this our aid which he is now enabled to bestow upon us all.

I group *Appearances* into ten as:

(i)   *To Mary of Magdala, otherwise that Mary out of whom he had cast seven devils (there were other women at this Appearance but I concentrate on this Mary).*

(ii)   *Also, sometime during that day to Simon Peter, or Cephas, the Rock.*

(iii)   *Perhaps almost simultaneously is that to Cleopas perhaps going home to Emmaus with another (possibly Simon) as indication of the company of disciples breaking up and so the Lord stays with them and breaks bread for the first time after his death. Recognising him, he vanishes and they immediately hurry the seven miles back to Galilee.*

(iv)	*Then, in the evening he appears to the eleven (without Thomas but with Matthias, Judas Iscariah having died in his Lord's service) as they are eating.*
(v) & (iv)	*It's now necessary to refer to 1 Corinthians 15 for his appearance to above five hundred brethren at once and separately to James*
(vii)	*Following that there is his appearance to 11 disciples on a mountain in Galilee, which I like to think may be the scene of the miracle of the five small loaves and two fishes by the lake's shore. I also suggest this is his appearance to "all the apostles" mentioned in 1 Corinthians 15 7 because they were no longer disciples having received at the first appearance to the 11 (see iv above) the gift of the Holy Spirit making them apostles, to which he first referred them as that in the loaves and fishes miracle. But, I just do not know.*
(viii)	*As in (vii) "some doubted", then his appearance 8 days after that first Easter Day to all 12 including Thomas must follow on afterwards.*
(ix)	*Next, by the Sea of Tiberius (otherwise Lake of Galilee) where some are individually named as:*
Simon Peter
Thomas Didymus
Nathaneal of Cana
The Sons of Zebedee (James and John)
And two others (could these be those first mentioned as the two on the way to Emmaus (Cleopas and Simon)
(x)	*Finally, to Paul, not forgetting the references to many other signs.*

After those Appearances, some will never see each other on Earth again. For example, on that first following Boxing Day, Stephen will become the first Martyr.

I concentrate upon the first four *Appearances* which are individual, one to one, being mystical experiences : Mary of Magdela, *first in faith*
                                                                Simon Peter,   *recanting*
                                                                Cleopas,   *returning*
                                                                Thomas,   *renouncing doubt*
to which I add as chorus Joseph of Arimathea (who tended his body). If it amounts to some poetic licence then I apologise but I seek a framework.

This Poem is one of Joy. The night of labour to salvation is passed. This is an interregnum for experiencing Resurrection before His disciples embark upon their mission.

One puzzlement to me is why after those first four, there are so few in the 40 days until Ascension, some six weeks later. Is it because there were just "so many signs" that it was common knowledge and hardly worth reportage.

So this is my 66 line poem in 22 stanzas of 3 lines of verse each to be spoken by 5 voices, in order of Appearance: Simon Peter
                                            Mary of Magdela
                                            Joseph of Arimathea
                                            Cleopas of Emmaus
                                            Thomas Didymus
and Peter has 21, Mary 18 and the other 3 have 9 lines each.

I wrote the Poem in my garden at Kintbury between Sunday 2nd and Sunday 23rd September 2007, an Indian Summer, of which we cannot have too many.

---

[1] *The Oxford Dictionary to the Christian Church* 3rd Edition Revised 2006 p 1397

Appearances

a piece for five voices

in order of appearance

Simon Peter
Mary of Magdela
Joseph of Arimathea
Cleopas of Emmaus
Thomas Didymus

figuring

Transfiguration
four appearances (with chorus)
Ascension

Transfiguration (Simon Peter)

into his high mountain separate and apart for prayer
talking together to Moses to Elijah to treasure
this our beloved who provides our whole pleasure

we blinded by his glittering garments rise without fear
in this appearance as his countenance changes to conversion
these secret *things* reveal to promises of resurrection

Appearance I (Mary of Magdela)

of weariness of early morning garden wandering
where rests his relics there my heart as Ruth's lies buried
of folded linen on bright angellic voices carried

this first day new week new centuries for blessing
through mist-filled eyes reveal me first in faith
Rabboni moving my imagination from your wraith

my spices waste away me seeking living not some dead
he touches me I need no touch of doubt no maudlin eye
unveils to me my golden domed Basilica at Vézelay

Chorus (Joseph of Arimathea)

I bear your body grieved by tombed Gethsemene
I roll and seal my stone with myrrh with alloes
I waiting for his kingdom expecting nothing no hallows

Appearance II (Simon Peter otherwise Cephas)

I renew his napkin wrapped separate as Turin's shroud
as denials threefold tinnitus drum ears nought else prevail
persistent woman's words may overcome my failed travail

much later by that lake which fed five thousand
from two small fish I cast my net to walk on water
to fish for men to still their fire for breaking bread for later

by lakeshore as I heard his far off call discipleship
renouncing my refusals to re-affirm his grace
I rock myself in Rome's Basilica my temporal resting place

Chorus (Joseph of Arimathea)

now we who wait attending on those prayer-full
mindful of our tasks our missionary endeavour
must first attend our flocks to minister their measure

Appearance III (Cleopas of Emmaus)

as weary on our way our sadness wearing heavy
returning homeless to Emmaus no longer housing home
as by our side speaks words of comfort hope and balm

now turning evenwards this day full spent
reciting texts of wisdom all that he has known
now vanishing feeds my heart and fills my empty soul

returning to those twelve his message heartening
this place of faith fulfilled our nets can never break
this harvest from our sea he never will forsake

Chorus (Joseph of Arimathea)

he ate with us broiled fish some honeycomb
he showed us hands full sore from suffering
he opened up our eyes his prophesies revealing

Appearance IV (Thomas Didymus)

my touch of proof belies my following fellowship
consumed by fear by doubt by worried circumstance
needful for each event my eyes' own evidence

in appearance all is revealed with no discordant doubt
making richer my belief my faults to sensitivity
believing in my heart appearances no longer signify

this first confession to my Lord's divinity
splits now all sides with spears of martyrdoms
revealing me as India's Apostle San Tome's rugged cross

Chorus (Mary of Magdela)

new day eternal daylight
crossing full eastern skies with crescent freshness
gold on orange as all around Holy Spirit shall caress

each morning's sky colours away every evening's sacred
proclamation of salvation's eternal peace
in certainty of which nothing withstands without reach

in fellowship messages opening out to fold all others in
as brothers following this new age commandment as
in appearances new wisdoms which each new messenger has

Ascension (Simon Peter)

by his hillside by Bethany's close-knit homestead
see skies all firmaments opened and my Lord ascend
exchanging every power from heaven to earth descend

when filled with Holy Spirit's power I will fulfil his *Word*
in tongues which trip past comprehension
I pausing only for redemption through his passion

amen

On Leaving

And when he was yet afar, his father saw him and was stirred by mercy. And he ran and fell on his neck, and kissed him. And the son said to him, Father, I have sinned into heaven and before thee, and now I am not worthy to be called thy son. And the father said to his servants, Swithy, bring ye forth the first stole and clothe ye him, and give ye a ring in his hand and shoes on his feet. And bring ye a fat calf and slay ye, and eat we and make we feast. For this my son was dead, and has lived again. He perished, and is found.

The Wycliffe New Testament (1388) W.R. Cooper for the Tyndale Society, The British Library 2002, Luke XVvv 20 – 24.